CGP – we put the 'pro' into pronoun!

This fantastic CGP book is the best way to help pupils master Year 5 Spelling, Punctuation and Grammar.

It's packed with bite-sized bursts of practice at the perfect level for Year 5 pupils, and there's a fun puzzle at the end of each section.

We've included full answers to every question, and a handy progress chart to make marking a breeze!

What CGP is all about

Our sole aim here at CGP is to produce the highest quality books — carefully written, immaculately presented and dangerously close to being funny.

Then we work our socks off to get them out to you — at the cheapest possible prices.

Contents

Grammar

Grammar Test 1 2
Grammar Test 2 5
Grammar Test 3 8
Grammar Test 4 11
Grammar Puzzle 14

Punctuation

Punctuation Test 1 15
Punctuation Test 2 18
Punctuation Test 3 21
Punctuation Test 4 24
Punctuation Puzzle 27

Spelling

Spelling Test 1 28
Spelling Test 2 31
Spelling Test 3 34
Spelling Test 4 37
Spelling Puzzle 40

Mixed Practice

Mixed Practice Test 1 41
Mixed Practice Test 2 44
Mixed Practice Test 3 47
Mixed Practice Test 4 50
Mixed Practice Puzzle 53

Answers 54
Progress Chart 62

Published by CGP

Editors: Andy Cashmore, Emma Crighton, Catherine Heygate, Adam Worster
With thanks to Harriet Foster, Becca Lakin and Hannah Roscoe for the proofreading.
With thanks to Jan Greenway for the copyright research.

ISBN: 978 1 78908 674 4
Clipart from Corel®
Printed by Elanders Ltd, Newcastle upon Tyne.
Based on the classic CGP style created by Richard Parsons.

Text, design, layout and original illustrations © Coordination Group Publications Ltd. (CGP) 2020
All rights reserved.

**Photocopying this book is not permitted, even if you have a CLA licence.
Extra copies are available from CGP with next day delivery • 0800 1712 712 • www.cgpbooks.co.uk**

Grammar Test 1

Warm up

1. Circle the correct option to complete the sentence below in the **present tense**.

   I (forget / forgot) that we need to sweep the floor regularly.

   1 mark

2. Write the correct **pronoun** on the line to replace the words in **bold**.

   Rose baked her brother a cake for his birthday.

   Unfortunately, **her brother** didn't like it. ....

   1 mark

3. Tick the sentence below that is written in **Standard English**.
   Tick only **one** box.

   She's not seen none of the answers yet. ☐

   He didn't do nothing to help me out. ☐

   The schools have rejected the free computers. ☐

   1 mark

4. Underline the **conjunctions** in the sentences below.

   We'll have pizza for dinner and watch a film.

   I could bring popcorn later, or I could make a cake.

   2 marks

5. Tick **two** sentences below which contain a **modal verb**.

I must remember to wash my pyjamas. ☐

Have Kim and Hattie met each other yet? ☐

She was able to use the trampoline in the garden. ☐

I should build a robot to help with the cooking. ☐

2 marks

6. Join the sentences together using a suitable **conjunction**.

The enormous bird flew slowly. It landed on Tamar's chimney.

....

....

1 mark

7. Underline the **relative clause** in the sentence below, then write the **relative pronoun** on the line.

I spoke to the referee whose whistle went missing.

Relative pronoun: ....

2 marks

8. The passage below is missing some **adverbials**.
   Fill in the gaps with the correct adverbials. Use each option **once**.

   | Tomorrow   Unfortunately   In the afternoon |

   .... , I plan to spend the day at my favourite place in the world — Laychester Cove.

   .... , I'll buy an ice cream from the little kiosk on Laychester pier.

   .... , I can only stay until the early evening — I need to get home in time for tea.

   2 marks

9. Underline **two adverbs** in the sentence below.

   Mark and Samin have a chess lesson soon, so they need to think about whether they have time to play netball too.

   2 marks

   END OF TEST

   / 14

Grammar Test 2

Warm up

1. Which word in the sentence below is an **adjective**? Circle **one** box.

    At the zoo, there are several meerkats and one lonely panda.

    | At | several | lonely |

    1 mark

2. Circle the correct option to complete the sentence below in **Standard English**.

    Is one of (those / them) cakes for me, or are they all yours?

    1 mark

3. Circle the **relative pronoun** below.

    whether   which   why   what   would

    1 mark

4. Tick the sentence below where the underlined words are an **adverbial**. Tick only **one** box.

    <u>Due to lack of interest</u>, the fair is cancelled. ☐

    Abe, <u>the youngest sibling</u>, is the most mature. ☐

    <u>I am not allowed</u> to use sharp knives. ☐

    1 mark

5. Rewrite the sentence below so that it is in the **past perfect**.
Only change **one** word in the sentence.

I have forgotten my grandad's birthday.

....

1 mark

6. Join each pair of sentences together using a suitable **conjunction**.

I'm late. The bus got stuck in traffic.

....

....

I don't enjoy tennis. I love badminton.

....

....

2 marks

7. What type of **clause** is underlined in the sentence below?
Write your answer on the line.

Although she was afraid of heights, <u>she loved rock climbing</u>.

....

1 mark

8. Put a tick in each row to show whether the underlined word is an **adjective** or an **adverb**.

	Adjective	Adverb
It's <u>probably</u> safer to stay here.		
Here are two <u>possible</u> options.		
<u>Perhaps</u> Enji can build us a ship.		

3 marks

9. Fill in the gap in the sentence below with a suitable **modal verb**.

Mrs Shah asked if I ………………………… like

any help with my maths homework.

1 mark

10. Underline **two preposition phrases** in the passage below.

Yesterday, my best friend Nina showed me something — her new pet tortoises! One tortoise was shy and hid under the table, but the other one was very friendly and ate strawberries from my hand.

2 marks

END OF TEST

/ 14

Grammar Test 3

Warm up

1. Tick the sentence below that is written in **Standard English**. Tick only **one** box.

   I aren't afraid of ghosts. ☐

   We done the wrong thing. ☐

   I swam under the bridge. ☐

   1 mark

2. Circle the **conjunction** in the sentence below.

   Whenever you visit, my biscuit supplies run out quickly.

   1 mark

3. In the sentence below, what **word class** does the underlined word belong to? Circle **one** box.

   After I lost my ice skates, Jack lent me his.

   | possessive pronoun | verb | determiner | noun |

   1 mark

4. Rewrite the sentence below so that the **relative clause** **doesn't** start with a **relative pronoun**.

   Chris forgot to bring the book that I lent him.

   ....

   1 mark

5. Circle the correct options to complete the sentences below in the **past progressive**.

    Malia (is / was) giving out today's newspaper to her friends.

    Gavin and Lyra (are / were) playing board games this morning.

    2 marks

6. In the sentence below, underline the **adverb** which shows something is **certain**.

    I will definitely buy you something nice for Christmas this year.

    1 mark

7. Tick the sentence below which **doesn't** contain a **determiner**. Tick only **one** box.

    My stepsister and her husband recently bought puppies. ☐

    Badly built houses almost always collapse in the end. ☐

    Sloths are known for being lazy, but they aren't really. ☐

    1 mark

8. Complete each sentence by adding a **relative clause**.

    Elsa, ………………………………… , smiled at me.

    We went to the beach ………………………………… .

    2 marks

9. The passage below is missing some **adverbs**.
Fill in the gaps with suitable adverbs so that the text flows better.

> It is very easy to make salt dough in your kitchen at home.
>
> .... , you need to mix together flour,
>
> salt and water. Next, shape it into anything you like.
>
> .... , you'll need to bake it in the
>
> oven — ask an adult to help you with this.

2 marks

10. Rewrite these sentences, changing the verbs in brackets
so that the sentences are in the **present perfect**.

We + (to have) + (to unlock) + the cellar door.

....

Kie + (to have) + (to fly) + a plane to Morocco.

....

2 marks

END OF TEST

/ 14

Grammar Test 4

Warm up

1. Circle the verb below that is in the **simple past tense**.

   I was afraid of spiders, but now I know that they are harmless.

   1 mark

2. Is the group of words below a **phrase** or a **clause**?
   Write your answer on the line.

   under the willow tree

   ....

   1 mark

3. Which of these words can be used as a **preposition**?
   Circle **one** box.

   | during | there | ours | when |

   1 mark

4. Draw lines to match each sentence to the missing **pronoun**.

   | Mr Rheinhardt and .... visited the zoo. | | I |

   | Will you play with Suzannah and .... ? | | me |

   1 mark

5. Write **two** sentences, one in which '**break**' is used as a **noun** and one in which it is used as a **verb**.

   Noun: ....

   Verb: ....

   2 marks

6. Underline the **subordinate clause** in each sentence below.

   After working hard, the builders took a long nap.

   Sana needed more milk before she could make the tea.

   2 marks

7. Tick the sentence below where the **adverbial** has been underlined **incorrectly**. Tick only **one** box.

   Nick and Martin have been saving up <u>for a new house</u>. ☐

   <u>Last Wednesday</u>, they bought a nice cosy bungalow. ☐

   <u>Unfortunately</u> for Nick, Martin hopes to paint it yellow. ☐

   1 mark

8. Underline the **longest noun phrase** in the sentence below.

   Even now, the mysterious Loch Ness monster still fascinates the countless tourists who visit the Scottish Highlands.

   1 mark

9. Tick **two** sentences below which use the **present progressive**.

My dream was to live on a farm in the countryside. ☐

I was making a pair of curtains with my sewing machine. ☐

Despite the weather, Larry is planning to go for a walk. ☐

We are dancing in the semi-final tonight. ☐

2 marks

10. Rewrite the passage below. Replace **two** of the **nouns** with **pronouns** to make the text flow better.

Jemma learnt how to dive last year, and it rapidly became Jemma's favourite hobby. Her brother Sam doesn't enjoy diving as much, so Sam rarely goes on family diving trips.

....

....

....

....

2 marks

END OF TEST

/ 14

Grammar Puzzle

This puzzle is a brilliant way to practise your grammar skills.

Carla's Conundrum

Carla has received a letter from one of her friends with a secret message in it. In each line, circle the word that is an example of the word type in the box. Then rearrange the circled words to find the secret message.

Dear Carla,

I thought you should know that I am going — **modal verb**

to learn Spanish over the summer holidays. — **verb**

A neighbour of mine named Juan can speak — **determiner**

the language and is going to teach me. I will — **noun**

also teach him some new words in English. I — **adjective**

hope to see you soon! — **pronoun**

From,
Taylor

The secret message is:

You should learn a new language.

Punctuation Test 1

Warm up

1. Tick the sentence that uses **capital letters** correctly.
Tick only **one** box.

   On thursday, Gary and Lisa are flying to Berlin. ☐

   my sister, Ivanka, is learning to speak Russian. ☐

   Every September, I go on holiday to Cornwall. ☐

   1 mark

2. Cross out the **incorrect comma** in the sentence below.

   After lunch, I often have a short, nap.

   1 mark

3. Draw lines to match each sentence to the missing punctuation mark.

What an extraordinary hat that is	!
I have a large collection of hats	?
Is Niall's hat too big for him	.

   2 marks

4. Tick **two** sentences that use **apostrophes** correctly.

Put your coat on — it's very cold outside. ☐

She put the guinea pig back in it's cage. ☐

The puppy wagged its tail when I stroked it. ☐

I don't know why its chasing me. ☐

2 marks

5. Rewrite the sentence below, adding the **extra information** in the box. Use **commas** where they are needed.

My brother is learning to drive. | who is seventeen |

....

....

1 mark

6. Read the passage below.

> The inhabitants of Little Middlington received a rather unusual visitor yesterday. Bella Briddlington of Twiddlington Close was watering her prize-winning cauliflowers when she discovered a giant panda grazing in her vegetable patch.

Write a suitable **heading** for this text.

....

1 mark

7. Add a **comma** in the correct place in each sentence below.

   Before I ate my lunch I washed my hands.

   As soon as the gates opened we all rushed inside.

   2 marks

8. Add one or more **commas** to each sentence so that it matches the meaning in the box **below** it.

   After they left Harry Li and Priyan went to the park.

   | All three children went to the park. |

   After they left Harry Li and Priyan went to the park.

   | Only Li and Priyan went to the park. |

   2 marks

9. What is the name of the punctuation used around 'Mr Harris' below?

   My teacher (Mr Harris) won the egg-and-spoon race.

   ....

   Explain why this punctuation has been used in this sentence.

   ....

   2 marks

END OF TEST

/ 14

Punctuation Test 2

Warm up

1. Underline the word that should have an **apostrophe**.

   My friends were surprised when they saw my dads new shoes.

   1 mark

2. This sentence is missing one **bracket**. Put it in the correct box.

   The church (built ☐ in 1902 ☐ needs ☐ a new ☐ roof.

   1 mark

3. Underline **two** words that are **missing** a **capital letter**.

   My friend Lucille lived in paris until last September, so

   she speaks french fluently. When she comes round next

   Monday, I hope she will teach me some useful phrases.

   2 marks

4. Tick the sentence that uses **commas incorrectly**.
   Tick only **one** box.

   Despite its big teeth, the crocodile seemed friendly. ☐

   At the supermarket I bought, three lemons and a kettle. ☐

   All of a sudden, James leapt up and raced outside. ☐

   1 mark

5. Add **two commas** to the sentence below so that is punctuated correctly.

   Sunita's hobbies include knitting outfits for her pet tarantula making sculptures from jelly extreme chess and open water swimming.

   2 marks

6. Rewrite each sentence in the correct order using a pair of **dashes**.

   | who is a vet | works with giraffes | my auntie |

   ....

   | was delicious | a type of pudding | her pavlova |

   ....

   2 marks

7. Rewrite the sentence below, adding a **comma** in the correct place.

   Although I like most sports I don't really enjoy rugby.

   ....

   ....

   1 mark

8. Put **inverted commas** in the correct places in the sentences below.

Are we nearly there yet ? asked Ollie hopefully .

Laila yelled , There's something behind you !

2 marks

9. Draw lines to match each paragraph to the most suitable **subheading**.

| Unlike most birds, kiwis cannot fly. Their tiny wings are too small to lift them into the air. |

Sniffing Out Snacks

| Most kiwis are nocturnal. They sleep during the day and are active at night. |

Feet On The Ground

| Kiwis are the only birds with nostrils at the end of their beaks. Their excellent sense of smell helps them to find food. |

Daytime Dozers

2 marks

END OF TEST

/ 14

Punctuation Test 3

Warm up

1. Tick the sentence that is punctuated correctly.
   Tick only **one** box.

   I always brush my teeth before bed. ☐

   What a fantastic outing that was? ☐

   Alfie took his tortoise for a walk ☐

   1 mark

2. Cross out the **incorrect comma** in the sentence below.

   My favourite trainers, the pink ones, are covered, in mud.

   1 mark

3. Tick the sentence that is punctuated correctly. Tick only **one** box.

   "Hang on" called Jakub, "I'll come with you." ☐

   Mrs Norris announced, "It's time to get ready for PE." ☐

   "Don't worry. We'll find it soon", Hafsah said. ☐

   1 mark

4. Add one set of **brackets** to the sentence below.

   Even my mum a very tall woman couldn't reach it .

   1 mark

5. Rewrite the phrases below using **possessive apostrophes**.

the coats belonging to Xavier

....

the books belonging to the people

....

2 marks

6. Tick the sentence that uses **commas incorrectly**.
Tick only **one** box.

We brought cheese and pickle sandwiches, cheese and onion crisps, cheese straws and a cheesecake. ☐

My mouse, Mr Nibbles, loves eating cheese. ☐

In the back, garden the gnomes are whistling loudly. ☐

1 mark

7. Rewrite the **incorrect** sentence from question 6 with the correct punctuation.

....

....

1 mark

8. Add a **comma** to each sentence below to change its meaning.

   Shall we race Amelia?

   Chuka likes painting his pets and volleyball.

   2 marks

9. Put **three** paragraph markers (//) in the passage below to show where new paragraphs should start.

   Amy closed her eyes and made a wish. Then, she took a deep breath and blew out all the candles on the cake. Amy's stepdad, Nigel, was standing on the other side of the room. He beamed at Amy and gave her a thumbs up. Two hours earlier, Nigel hadn't been looking quite so cheerful. Somehow, he had set fire to the first cake and dropped the second. The third had been more successful, although Nigel had made a slight mix-up with the salt and sugar. There hadn't been time to make a fourth. "Let's not cut the cake just yet, eh Amy?" Nigel suggested.

   3 marks

10. Rewrite the sentence below using **inverted commas** and the **correct punctuation**.

    I wonder said Poppy where my socks are

    ....

    1 mark

END OF TEST

/ 14

Punctuation Test 4

Warm up

1. This sentence is missing one **comma**. Put it in the correct box.

   Once ☐ it got ☐ dark ☐ we got into ☐ our tent.

   1 mark

2. Tick the sentence that uses **dashes** correctly. Tick only **one** box.

   The baker — a very generous man — gave me a pork pie. ☐

   Jo Tan a famous poet visited — my school — yesterday. ☐

   When we arrived — three hours — late it was closed. ☐

   1 mark

3. Add the missing **inverted commas** to the sentence below.

   "That sandwich , said Idris , looks delicious ."

   1 mark

4. Add **full stops** to the passage below and circle any letters that should be **capitals**.

   Wastwater is located in the Lake District in Cumbria with a depth of more than 70 metres, it is the deepest lake in England the lake is surrounded by mountains, including England's two highest peaks, Scafell Pike and Scafell.

   2 marks

5. Why does the word in **bold** below use an **apostrophe**?

   He cannot remember what **he's** done with the car keys.

   ....

   ....

   1 mark

6. Write a **question** to match each of the answers given below.

   Q: ....

   A: Yes please — I'm really thirsty.

   Q: ....

   A: It's green and orange with a purple bobble on top.

   2 marks

7. Write the items in the list as a **sentence**, using **commas** in the correct places.

   I am going to ....

   ....

   ....

   ....

   My to-do list
   polish my unicycle
   visit Uncle Bob
   feed the rabbits
   make some biscuits

   2 marks

8. Add an **apostrophe** to the underlined word in each sentence.

My <u>parents</u> names are Sarah and John.

I will mend this <u>bikes</u> brakes at the weekend.

The <u>horses</u> tails were all different lengths.

3 marks

9. Read the two sentences below. Explain how the **meaning** of the first sentence is **different** from the meaning of the second sentence.

Michal played the piano loudly, singing as he played.

Michal played the piano, loudly singing as he played.

....

....

....

1 mark

END OF TEST

/ 14

Punctuation Puzzle

This puzzle is a brilliant way to practise your punctuation skills.

Woeful Wizardry

Walter the Wizard has forgotten the magic word that will make his rabbit, Snuffles, disappear. Can you help him find it? Circle the sentences below that are punctuated correctly. Then, jot down the first letter of each sentence you've circled in the box below, and unscramble them to reveal the magic word.

"Can you help me find the magic word?" pleaded Walter.

Walter's magic word isn't wand, vanish or, poof.

Although Walter's forgetful, he's quite a good wizard.

Olivia (Walter's best friend) can't remember the magic word either.

Do you know how to make a rabbit vanish!

Right now, Snuffles is preparing to have a nap in Walter's favourite hat.

Its not easy to make any creature — even a rabbit — disappear.

"This isn't the only magic word that Walter has forgotten," said Olivia.

Snuffles, who's a very clever rabbit knows the magic word.

Rabbits, rhinos, raccoons and rats are some of Walter's favourite animals.

Letters:

The magic word is:

Spelling Test 1

Warm up

1. Add a **suffix** to the word in **bold** so that the sentence makes sense.

   I think I'll do some **garden**.................... later.

   1 mark

2. Circle the correct option to complete the sentence below.

   He walked to the shops, singing (merrily / merryly).

   1 mark

3. Circle the group of letters that is missing from **all** the words below.

   c........   th........t   br........t

   | ouh | | or | | ough |

   1 mark

4. Tick **two** sentences below which contain a spelling mistake.

   Gianne and Louise were absent from school. ☐

   That distence is too far for any dog to run. ☐

   The pregnant tiger stretched under the tree. ☐

   Her patiance was wearing thin by the end. ☐

   2 marks

5. Circle **one** word below that is spelt **incorrectly**.

embark   plaque   grotesk   mosque

1 mark

6. Rewrite the sentence below, correcting **one** spelling mistake.

Shanice was gradualy gaining on first place.

....

....

1 mark

7. Rewrite the words below as verbs, using the suffixes '**ate**', '**ise**' or '**ify**'.

You may need to change the spelling of the root word.

class   ....

active   ....

energy   ....

3 marks

8. Underline **two** spelling mistakes in the passage below.

> "I think you owe me an explanation," said Kyle, who was the owner of the resteurant where Annabel worked.
>
> Annabel shrugged awkwardly.
>
> "It's not my fault that the guests complained," she said. "As I've frequentely told you, it's a terrible idea to put marmalade in the vegetable soup."

2 marks

9. Rewrite the sentences below, correcting **two** spelling mistakes.

The magision was preparing for her performance. She gave me permition to watch while she got her props into position.

....

....

....

2 marks

END OF TEST

/ 14

Spelling Test 2

Warm up

1. Circle **one** word below that is spelt correctly.

   mythology   indecisyve   unymaginable

   _____ 1 mark

2. Underline **one** word that is spelt **incorrectly**.

   irresponsibly   visibly   sensably   probably

   _____ 1 mark

3. Draw lines to match each word to the correct **silent letter**.

   ....nives   t

   ....nomes   g

   this........le   k

   _____ 2 marks

4. Tick the sentence below which contains a spelling mistake.
   Tick only **one** box.

   It's probable that this elephant is from India. ☐

   You're unbelievible sometimes, Jared. ☐

   Sophie's best score was unbeatable. ☐

   _____ 1 mark

5. The prefix '**re**' can be added to '**adjust**'.
   What does '**readjust**' mean? Tick only **one** box.

   to adjust carefully ☐

   to adjust again ☐

   to adjust incorrectly ☐

   1 mark

6. Rewrite the sentence below, correcting **one** spelling mistake.

   Sheila's absolutely exsellent at throwing surprise parties.

   ....

   ....

   1 mark

7. Rewrite each word below, adding the suffix '**ous**' or '**ation**'.

   You may need to change the spelling of the root word.

disaster	....
prepare	....
adore	....
outrage	....

   4 marks

8. Underline **one** spelling mistake in the sentence below.

   Grant had always been fasinated by science and technology.

   1 mark

9. The prefix '**dis**' can be added to '**appear**' to make '**disappear**'. Explain how the **prefix** changes the **meaning** of the word.

   ....

   ....

   1 mark

10. Underline **one** spelling mistake in the passage below.

    After cycling down the track for a few minutes, I reached a farm. There was a horse in one of the fields, so I dismounted, said hello and stroked its main for a while. It was very friendly — I hope we meet again one day.

    1 mark

END OF TEST

/ 14

Spelling Test 3

Warm up

1. Tick the word below which is spelt correctly.
   Tick only **one** box.

   distroust ☐   couple ☐   hiccoup ☐

   _____
   1 mark

2. Underline the word where '**ch**' sounds like a hard '**c**' sound.

   The chandelier crashed to the ground, causing

   chaos among the crowd of charming children.

   _____
   1 mark

3. Complete the words in the passage below using the options from the box.

   | ei   eigh   ey |

   I gently pulled on the r..............ns of my horse,

   Molly. She n..............ed softly and gradually came

   to a halt. Molly's mane is wonderfully soft and is a

   light gr.............. colour. I stroked her neck before

   encouraging her forward for the last part of our ride.

   _____
   2 marks

4. Draw lines to match each word beginning to the correct ending.

spa........

preten........

ambi........

cious

tious

3 marks

5. Circle the word where '**ough**' is pronounced like the word '**oh**'.

nought   rough   dough

1 mark

6. Write down **one** other word where '**ough**' is pronounced like the word '**oh**'.

....

1 mark

7. Rewrite the sentence below, correcting **one** spelling mistake.

Yesterday, Isa lead us in the ascent of a dangerous mountain.

....

....

1 mark

8. Tick the sentence below which contains a spelling mistake.
    Tick only **one** box.

    The referee gave her a red card. ☐

    I have been refered to a new doctor. ☐

    The reference book was old and dusty. ☐

    _____
    1 mark

9. Circle **one** word to complete the sentence below.

    The storm will .... our plans to go sailing.

    | affect | | effect |

    _____
    1 mark

10. Underline **two** words below that are spelt **incorrectly**.
    Then write the correct spellings on the dotted lines.

    creatcher   culture   richer   departure

    gesture   leizure   pleasure   stretcher

    ....

    ....

    _____
    2 marks

END OF TEST

/ 14

Spelling Test 4

Warm up

1. Add a **prefix** to the word in **bold** so that the sentence makes sense.

   The ....**marine** was found at the bottom of the ocean.

   1 mark

2. Underline **one** spelling mistake in the sentence below.

   Maya had to make a difficult decician during the match.

   1 mark

3. Circle **one** word below that is spelt **incorrectly**.

   | machine | chalet | broshure | sherbet |

   1 mark

4. Tick the sentence below which contains a spelling mistake.
   Tick only **one** box.

   The wolf was incredibly vicious. ☐

   His loud laughter was infectious. ☐

   Mike ate the delitious cake in one go. ☐

   1 mark

5. Circle the correct spellings to complete the sentences below.

   Jabir was (essential / essencial) to the mission's success.

   Exercise can be (benefitial / beneficial) for your health.

   2 marks

6. Draw lines to match each **prefix** to the correct word.

ir		mortal
im		reversible
il		legible

   2 marks

7. Rewrite the sentence below, correcting **one** spelling mistake.

   The business was famous for making peculier lamps.

   ....

   ....

   1 mark

8. Underline the word below that is spelt **incorrectly**.
   Then write the correct spelling on the dotted line.

   preferrence   transferred   deferred

   ....

   1 mark

9. Underline **two** spelling mistakes in the passage below.

> The detective sat me down and asked me to discribe the person who had stolen the bicycle.
>
> "She was a tall individual with long blonde hair, and she looked about fourty years old."
>
> "Did you see where she went?" the detective asked.
>
> "She rode the bike through the cemetery."

2 marks

10. Underline **two** words below that are spelt **incorrectly**.
    Then write the correct spellings on the dotted lines.

    receive   siege   retrieve   percieve

    conceive   sheild   sieve   ceiling

    ....

    ....

2 marks

END OF TEST

/ 14

Spelling Puzzle

This puzzle is a brilliant way to practise your spelling skills.

Petey's Plunder

Petey the Pirate has dug up a chest full of coins, but he needs a code word to unlock it. Use the clues below to complete the crossword, then unscramble the letters in the white squares to find out the word for the chest.

Across

1. Land that is surrounded by an ocean.
4. What pirates often find in chests buried underground.
7. Valuable or important.
8. To measure how heavy something is.

Down

2. Where your food goes to be digested.
3. Sunny and windy are types of this.
4. An idea in your mind.
5. The ability to lift heavy things.
6. Difficult or tricky.

The code word for the chest is:

Mixed Practice Test 1

Warm up

1. Tick the sentence below that is written in **Standard English**.
   Tick only **one** box.

   The invitation was addressed to my brother and me. ☐

   I'll take them clothes to the charity shop tomorrow. ☐

   An umbrella won't do you no good in this wind. ☐

   1 mark

2. In the sentence below, what **word class** does the underlined word belong to? Circle **one** box.

   We accidentally kicked the football <u>into</u> our neighbour's garden.

   | adverb | preposition | determiner | noun |

   1 mark

3. Add **one comma** to the sentence below so that it is punctuated correctly.

   Riley found it hard to sleep because of the icy draught blowing under the door his incredibly uncomfortable pillow and the furious bird that was squawking at the foot of his bed.

   1 mark

4. Draw lines to match each **prefix** to the correct word.

super		graph
auto		merged
sub		star

2 marks

5. Tick **two** sentences where the **apostrophe** shows **possession**.

Julia's going to play outside with Freya and Amit. ☐

I am not allowed to go into my sister's bedroom. ☐

After school, we took Charlotte's goldfish to the vet. ☐

I think our teacher's planning a surprise for us. ☐

2 marks

6. Write a **subordinate clause** to complete each of these sentences. Use a different **subordinating conjunction** each time.

My teacher gave me a gold star ....

....

Maisie mowed the lawn ....

....

2 marks

7. Underline the **modal verb** in the sentence below.

   Josh said that he might come to the cinema with us if he finishes his homework in time.

   1 mark

8. Draw lines to show whether the sentences below are in the **present progressive**, the **present perfect** or the **past perfect**.

We had won the match.	**present progressive**
They have been here before.	**present perfect**
She is writing a letter to him.	**past perfect**

   2 marks

9. Rewrite the sentence below, correcting **two** spelling mistakes.

   Fatima couldn't beleive her eyes when she saw all the equippment in the science laboratory at her new school.

   ....

   ....

   ....

   2 marks

END OF TEST

/ 14

Mixed Practice Test 2

Warm up

1. Circle **one noun** in the sentence below.

   Mr Bence struggled to contain his intense anger.

   1 mark

2. This sentence is missing **one dash**. Put it in the correct box.

   That ☐ hat ☐ the red one — is ☐ too small ☐ for me.

   1 mark

3. Tick the sentence that contains a **possessive pronoun**.
   Tick only **one** box.

   Tamsin was excited to visit her dad. ☐

   If the boots don't fit, he can borrow mine. ☐

   Will they like the cake we got for them? ☐

   1 mark

4. Circle the correct spellings to complete the sentences below.

   A donkey trotted past, (wistling / whistling) quietly to itself.

   Darryl poked the pudding (suspiciously / suspitiously).

   2 marks

5. Underline **two determiners** in the sentence below.

I am trying to find the seagull that stole my sandwich.

2 marks

6. Put a tick in each row to show whether the words are a **noun phrase** or a **preposition phrase**.

	Noun Phrase	Preposition Phrase
in my bedroom		
the big green frog		
behind our recycling box		

3 marks

7. Underline **two** spelling mistakes in the passage below.

During the summer holidays, my family and I love going on advensures. Last year, we visited a shark-infested cave at the bottom of the ocean. This year, we are planning an even more extreme experience involving parashutes and dinosaurs.

2 marks

8. Rewrite the sentence below, replacing the adverb in **bold** with one that is **more certain**.

   Megan overslept, so she will **probably** be late.

   ....

   ....

   1 mark

9. Read the two sentences below. Explain how the **meaning** of the first sentence is **different** from the meaning of the second sentence.

   The witch, who flew past my window, frequently lost her broomstick.

   The witch, who flew past my window frequently, lost her broomstick.

   ....

   ....

   ....

   1 mark

END OF TEST

/ 14

Mixed Practice Test 3

Warm up

1. Circle **one** word below that is spelt **incorrectly**.

   afraid   obay   weight

   1 mark

2. Add **full stops** to the passage below and circle any letters that should be **capitals**.

   Mrs Lang has several unusual pets the strangest is Kenny, who is a cross between a crocodile and a horse he looks very unusual indeed.

   2 marks

3. Tick **two** sentences below that contain a spelling mistake.

   I like all kinds of music, but percusion is my favourite. ☐

   Mya's latest invention is a robotic dog called Fluffy. ☐

   Luke suddenly realised that he had forgotten his shoes. ☐

   Will your grandad be attendding parents' evening? ☐

   2 marks

4. Underline the **relative clause** in the sentence below, then write the **relative pronoun** on the line.

These are the gloves that Ruby gave me for Christmas.

Relative pronoun: ....

2 marks

5. Draw lines to match each sentence on the **left** to a sentence on the **right** that belongs in the same **paragraph**.

| Filip got a new bike for his tenth birthday. | They played two games, then had pancakes for tea. |

| One day, Filip cycled to Auntie Edna's house and played chess with her. | A sign said the road was closed, but Filip ignored it. |

| On the way home, Filip took a shortcut along a back road. | It was bright red with blue handlebars and a blue saddle. |

2 marks

6. Tick the sentence below where the underlined words are a **main clause**. Tick only **one** box.

   I like ham in my sandwiches, but <u>Phoebe prefers jam</u>. ☐

   <u>Even though Jen isn't very fast</u>, she won the race. ☐

   He wanted to bake <u>the biggest apple pie in the world</u>. ☐

   1 mark

7. Rewrite the sentences below so that they are in the **past progressive**. Only change **one** word in each sentence.

   Sarita and Ben are playing hockey.

   ....

   My mum is painting the garage.

   ....

   2 marks

8. Underline **two** words below that are spelt **incorrectly**. Then write the correct spellings on the dotted lines.

   violence   influential   artifitial   evidence

   social   performance   official   substance

   ....

   2 marks

END OF TEST

/ 14

Mixed Practice Test 4

Warm up

1. Tick the sentence that uses **brackets** correctly. Tick only **one** box.

   Henry VIII a king of England was born (in 1491). ☐

   My stepsister (who is an astronaut) lives on Mars. ☐

   We were going to have a barbecue (but it rained). ☐

   1 mark

2. Add a **suffix** to the word in **bold** so that the sentence makes sense.

   I made a poster to **advert**.................... the school fair.

   1 mark

3. Write the correct **pronoun** on each line to replace the words in **bold**.

   Tony finished his soup, but **Tony** also wanted a pie.   ....

   Sara had eaten his pie and **the pie** was delicious.   ....

   2 marks

4. Rewrite the sentence below so that it starts with the **adverbial**. Remember to use the correct **punctuation**.

   We enjoyed our trip despite the terrible weather.

   ....

   ....

   1 mark

5. Underline **one** spelling mistake in the sentence below, then write the **correct** spelling on the line.

My friends were full of admireation when my rabbit performed the trick I had taught him.

....

1 mark

6. Underline the **adverb** in the sentence below. Circle the **adjective**.

The elves sometimes get chilly in the winter.

2 marks

7. Put a tick in each row to show whether the sentence contains a **co-ordinating conjunction** or a **subordinating conjunction**.

	Co-ordinating Conjunction	Subordinating Conjunction
Kayla went shopping and bought a new mug.		
Before he went swimming, Adam had a snack.		
I stroked the cat even though I was scared of it.		

3 marks

8. Rewrite the sentence below using **inverted commas** and the **correct punctuation**.

I think yawned Oren it's time for bed

....

1 mark

9. Write each of these words in a sentence.

advice

....

....

advise

....

....

2 marks

END OF TEST

/ 14

Mixed Practice Puzzle

This puzzle is a brilliant way to practise your spelling, punctuation and grammar skills.

Quizzy Queen

The Queen of Quizzes has offered a reward to anyone who can answer her questions correctly. Follow the trail of questions and answer each one correctly to reach the reward.

1 Name one type of punctuation that can go around a parenthesis.

....

2 Solve the anagram: S P R U R S I E

....

3 Name the type of verb that can show how possible something is.

....

4 Solve the anagram: K H I N G T

....

5 Which punctuation marks go around direct speech?

....

6 True or false: adjectives describe verbs.

....

7 Solve the anagram: W O P U R F E L

....

8 True or false: 'who' is a relative pronoun.

....

© CGP — not to be photocopied   53   Mixed Practice Puzzle

Answers

Grammar Test 1 – pages 2-4

1. I **forget** that we need to sweep the floor regularly.
 (**1 mark**)
2. he
 (**1 mark**)
3. The schools have rejected the free computers.
 (**1 mark**)
4. We'll have pizza for dinner <u>and</u> watch a film.
 I could bring popcorn later, <u>or</u> I could make a cake.
 (**1 mark for 1 correct,
 2 marks for both correct**)
5. I must remember to wash my pyjamas.
 I should build a robot to help with the cooking.
 (**1 mark for 1 correct,
 2 marks for both correct**)
6. E.g. The enormous bird flew slowly **before** it landed on Tamar's chimney.
 (**1 mark for any sensible sentence that uses a conjunction**)
7. I spoke to the referee <u>whose whistle went missing</u>.
 Relative pronoun: whose
 (**1 mark for correctly underlining the relative clause, 1 mark for correctly identifying the relative pronoun**)
8. **Tomorrow**, I plan to spend the day at my favourite place in the world — Laychester Cove.
 In the afternoon, I'll buy an ice cream from the little kiosk on Laychester pier.
 Unfortunately, I can only stay until the early evening — I need to get home in time for tea.
 (**1 mark for 1 or 2 correct,
 2 marks for 3 correct**)
9. Mark and Samin have a chess lesson <u>soon</u>, so they need to think about whether they have time to play netball <u>too</u>.
 (**1 mark for 1 correct,
 2 marks for both correct**)

Grammar Test 2 – pages 5-7

1. lonely
 (**1 mark**)
2. Is one of **those** cakes for me, or are they all yours?
 (**1 mark**)
3. which
 (**1 mark**)
4. Due to lack of interest, the fair is cancelled.
 (**1 mark**)
5. I had forgotten my grandad's birthday.
 (**1 mark**)
6. E.g. I'm late **because** the bus got stuck in traffic.
 E.g. I don't enjoy tennis, **but** I love badminton.
 (**1 mark for each sensible sentence that uses a conjunction, up to 2 marks in total**)
7. main clause
 (**1 mark**)
8.

	Adjective	Adverb
It's <u>probably</u> safer to stay here.		✓
Here are two <u>possible</u> options.	✓	
<u>Perhaps</u> Enji can build us a ship.		✓

 (**1 mark for each correct,
 up to 3 marks in total**)
9. E.g. Mrs Shah asked if I **would** like any help with my maths homework.
 (**1 mark for any sensible modal verb**)
10. Yesterday, my best friend Nina showed me something — her new pet tortoises! One tortoise was shy and hid <u>under the table</u>, but the other one was very friendly and ate strawberries <u>from my hand</u>.
 (**1 mark for 1 correct,
 2 marks for both correct**)

Grammar Test 3 – pages 8-10

1. I swam under the bridge.
 (**1 mark**)
2. **Whenever** you visit, my biscuit supplies run out quickly.
 (**1 mark**)
3. possessive pronoun
 (**1 mark**)
4. Chris forgot to bring the book I lent him.
 (**1 mark**)

Answers

5. Malia **was** giving out today's newspaper to her friends.
   Gavin and Lyra **were** playing board games this morning.
   (**1 mark for 1 correct,
   2 marks for both correct**)

6. I will <u>definitely</u> buy you something nice for Christmas this year.
   (**1 mark**)

7. Sloths are known for being lazy, but they aren't **really**.
   (**1 mark**)

8. E.g. Elsa, **who is always cheerful**, smiled at me.
   E.g. We went to the beach **where we first met**.
   (**1 mark for each sensible relative clause, up to 2 marks in total**)

9. E.g. It is very easy to make salt dough in your kitchen at home. **Firstly**, you need to mix together flour, salt and water. Next, shape it into anything you like. **Finally**, you'll need to bake it in the oven — ask an adult to help you with this.
   (**1 mark for 1 sensible adverb,
   2 marks for 2 sensible adverbs**)

10. We have unlocked the cellar door.
    Kie has flown a plane to Morocco.
    (**1 mark for 1 correct,
    2 marks for both correct**)

Grammar Test 4 – pages 11-13

1. I **was** afraid of spiders, but now I know that they are harmless.
   (**1 mark**)

2. a phrase
   (**1 mark**)

3. during
   (**1 mark**)

4.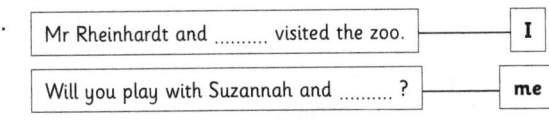
   (**1 mark for both correct**)

5. E.g. It's time to take a break.
   E.g. Break that chocolate bar in half.
   (**1 mark for any sensible sentence that uses 'break' as a noun, 1 mark for any sensible sentence that uses 'break' as a verb**)

6. <u>After working hard</u>, the builders took a long nap.
   Sana needed more milk <u>before she could make the tea</u>.
   (**1 mark for 1 correct,
   2 marks for both correct**)

7. Unfortunately for Nick, Martin hopes to paint it yellow.
   (**1 mark**)

8. Even now, the mysterious Loch Ness monster still fascinates <u>the countless tourists who visit the Scottish Highlands</u>.
   (**1 mark**)

9. Despite the weather, Larry is planning to go for a walk.
   We are dancing in the semi-final tonight.
   (**1 mark for 1 correct,
   2 marks for both correct**)

10. Jemma learnt how to dive last year, and it rapidly became **her** favourite hobby. Her brother Sam doesn't enjoy diving as much, so **he** rarely goes on family diving trips.
    (**1 mark for 1 pronoun correct,
    2 marks for both correct**)

Grammar Puzzle – page 14

You should have circled the words in bold:
I thought you **should** know that I am going to **learn** Spanish over the summer holidays. **A** neighbour of mine named Juan can speak the **language** and is going to teach me. I will also teach him some **new** words in English. I hope to see **you** soon!

The secret message is: You should learn a new language.

Punctuation Test 1 – pages 15-17

1. Every September, I go on holiday to Cornwall.
   (**1 mark**)

2. After lunch, I often have a short nap.
   (**1 mark**)

Answers

3. What an extraordinary hat that is — !
   I have a large collection of hats — .
   Is Niall's hat is too big for him — ?
   (**1 mark for 1 or 2 correct,
   2 marks for 3 correct**)

4. Put your coat on — it's very cold outside.
   The puppy wagged its tail when I stroked it.
   (**1 mark for 1 correct,
   2 marks for both correct**)

5. My brother, who is seventeen, is learning to drive.
   (**1 mark**)

6. E.g. Panda Discovered in Vegetable Patch
   (**1 mark for any sensible heading**)

7. Before I ate my lunch, I washed my hands.
   As soon as the gates opened, we all rushed inside.
   (**1 mark for 1 correct,
   2 marks for both correct**)

8. After they left, Harry, Li and Priyan went to the park.
   After they left Harry, Li and Priyan went to the park.
   (**1 mark for 1 sentence correct,
   2 marks for both correct**)

9. brackets
   E.g. They separate the extra information in the sentence.
   (**1 mark for 1 correct,
   2 marks for both correct**)

Punctuation Test 2 – pages 18-20

1. My friends were surprised when they saw my <u>dads</u> new shoes.
   (**1 mark**)

2. The church (built in 1902) needs a new roof.
   (**1 mark**)

3. My friend Lucille lived in <u>paris</u> until last September, so she speaks <u>french</u> fluently. When she comes round next Monday, I hope she will teach me some useful phrases.
   (**1 mark for 1 correct,
   2 marks for both correct**)

4. At the supermarket I bought, three lemons and a kettle.
   (**1 mark**)

5. Sunita's hobbies include knitting outfits for her pet tarantula, making sculptures from jelly, extreme chess and open water swimming.
   (**1 mark for 1 correct,
   2 marks for both correct**)

6. My auntie — who is a vet — works with giraffes.
   Her pavlova — a type of pudding — was delicious.
   (**1 mark for 1 sentence correct,
   2 marks for both correct**)

7. Although I like most sports, I don't really enjoy rugby.
   (**1 mark**)

8. "Are we nearly there yet?" asked Ollie hopefully.
   Laila yelled, "There's something behind you!"
   (**1 mark for 1 sentence correct,
   2 marks for both correct**)

9. Unlike most birds... — Feet On The Ground
   Most kiwis are nocturnal... — Daytime Dozers
   Kiwis are the only birds... — Sniffing Out Snacks
   (**1 mark for 1 or 2 correct,
   2 marks for 3 correct**)

Punctuation Test 3 – pages 21-23

1. I always brush my teeth before bed.
   (**1 mark**)

2. My favourite trainers, the pink ones, are covered in mud.
   (**1 mark**)

3. Mrs Norris announced, "It's time to get ready for PE."
   (**1 mark**)

4. Even my mum (a very tall woman) couldn't reach it.
   (**1 mark**)

5. Xavier's coats
   the people's books
   (**1 mark for 1 correct,
   2 marks for both correct**)

6. In the back, garden the gnomes are whistling loudly.
   (**1 mark**)

Answers

7. In the back garden, the gnomes are whistling loudly.
(**1 mark**)

8. Shall we race, Amelia?
Chuka likes painting, his pets and volleyball.
(**1 mark for 1 correct,
2 marks for both correct**)

9. Amy closed her eyes and made a wish. Then, she took a deep breath and blew out all the candles on the cake. // Amy's stepdad, Nigel, was standing on the other side of the room. He beamed at Amy and gave her a thumbs-up. // Two hours earlier, Nigel hadn't been looking quite so cheerful. Somehow, he had set fire to the first cake and dropped the second. The third had been more successful, although Nigel had made a slight mix-up with the salt and sugar. There hadn't been time to make a fourth. // "Let's not cut the cake just yet, eh Amy?" Nigel suggested.
(**1 mark for each correct,
up to 3 marks in total**)

10. "I wonder," said Poppy, "where my socks are."
(**1 mark**)

Punctuation Test 4 – pages 24-26

1. Once it got dark, we got into our tent.
(**1 mark**)

2. The baker — a very generous man — gave me a pork pie.
(**1 mark**)

3. "That sandwich," said Idris, "looks delicious."
(**1 mark**)

4. Wastwater is located in the Lake District in Cumbria. With a depth of more than 70 metres, it is the deepest lake in England. The lake is surrounded by mountains, including England's two highest peaks, Scafell Pike and Scafell.
(**1 mark for 1 full stop and 1 capital letter correct, 2 marks for all correct**)

5. E.g. To show that it is a contraction of 'he has'.
(**1 mark**)

6. E.g. Would you like a drink?
E.g. What does your hat look like?
(**1 mark for each sensible question, punctuated correctly, up to 2 marks in total**)

7. E.g. I am going to polish my unicycle, visit Uncle Bob, feed the rabbits and make some biscuits.
(**1 mark for each correctly positioned comma, up to 2 marks in total**)

8. My parents' names are Sarah and John.
I will mend this bike's brakes at the weekend.
The horses' tails were all different lengths.
(**1 mark for each correct,
up to 3 marks in total**)

9. E.g. In the first sentence, Michal was playing the piano loudly while he sang, but in the second sentence, Michal was singing loudly while he played the piano.
(**1 mark for any sensible answer**)

Punctuation Puzzle – page 27

You should have circled:
"**C**an you help me find the magic word?" pleaded Walter.
Although Walter's forgetful, he's quite a good wizard.
Olivia (Walter's best friend) can't remember the magic word either.
Right now, Snuffles is preparing to have a nap in Walter's favourite hat.
"**T**his isn't the only magic word that Walter has forgotten," said Olivia.
Rabbits, rhinos, raccoons and rats are some of Walter's favourite animals.

The magic word is carrot.

Spelling Test 1 – pages 28-30

1. I think I'll do some garden**ing** later.
(**1 mark**)

2. He walked to the shops, singing **merrily**.
(**1 mark**)

3. ough
(**1 mark**)

4. That dist**e**nce is too far for any dog to run.
Her pati**a**nce was wearing thin by the end.
(**1 mark for 1 correct,
2 marks for both correct**)

5. grotesk
(**1 mark**)

Answers

6. Shanice was **gradually** gaining on first place.
   (**1 mark**)
7. classify
   activate
   energise
   (**1 mark for each correct, up to 3 marks in total**)
8. "I think you owe me an explanation," said Kyle, who was the owner of the <u>resteurant</u> where Annabel worked.
   Annabel shrugged awkwardly.
   "It's not my fault that the guests complained," she said. "As I've <u>frequentely</u> told you, it's a terrible idea to put marmalade in the vegetable soup."
   (**1 mark for 1 correct, 2 marks for both correct**)
9. The **magician** was preparing for her performance. She gave me **permission** to watch while she got her props into position.
   (**1 mark for 1 correct, 2 marks for both correct**)

Spelling Test 2 – pages 31-33

1. mythology
   (**1 mark**)
2. sensably
   (**1 mark**)
3.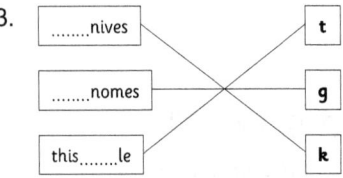

   (**1 mark for 1 or 2 correct, 2 marks for 3 correct**)
4. You're unbelievible sometimes, Jared.
   (**1 mark**)
5. to adjust again
   (**1 mark**)
6. Sheila's absolutely **excellent** at throwing surprise parties.
   (**1 mark**)
7. disastrous
   preparation
   adoration
   outrageous
   (**1 mark for each correct, up to 4 marks in total**)
8. Grant had always been <u>fasinated</u> by science and technology.
   (**1 mark**)
9. E.g. The prefix makes the word mean the opposite.
   (**1 mark for any sensible explanation**)
10. After cycling down the track for a few minutes, I reached a farm. There was a horse in one of the fields, so I dismounted, said hello and stroked its <u>main</u> for a while. It was very friendly — I hope we meet again one day.
    (**1 mark**)

Spelling Test 3 – pages 34-36

1. couple
   (**1 mark**)
2. The chandelier crashed to the ground, causing <u>chaos</u> among the crowd of charming children.
   (**1 mark**)
3. I gently pulled on the **reins** of my horse, Molly. She **neighed** softly and gradually came to a halt. Molly's mane is wonderfully soft and is a light **grey** colour. I stroked her neck before encouraging her forward for the last part of our ride.
   (**1 mark for 1 or 2 correct, 2 marks for 3 correct**)
4.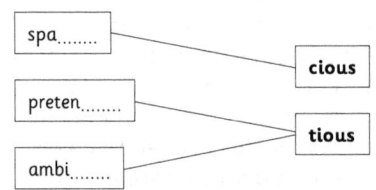

   (**1 mark for each correct, up to 3 marks in total**)
5. dough
   (**1 mark**)
6. E.g. though
   (**1 mark for any word where 'ough' is pronounced 'oh'**)

Answers

7. Yesterday, Isa **led** us in the ascent of a dangerous mountain.
(**1 mark**)
8. I have been refered to a new doctor.
(**1 mark**)
9. affect
(**1 mark**)
10. creatcher — creature
leizure — leisure
(**1 mark for 1 correct,
2 marks for both correct**)

Spelling Test 4 – pages 37-39

1. The **sub**marine was found at the bottom of the ocean.
(**1 mark**)
2. Maya had to make a difficult decician during the match.
(**1 mark**)
3. broshure
(**1 mark**)
4. Mike ate the delitious cake in one go.
(**1 mark**)
5. Jabir was **essential** to the mission's success. Exercise can be **beneficial** for your health.
(**1 mark for 1 correct,
2 marks for both correct**)
6.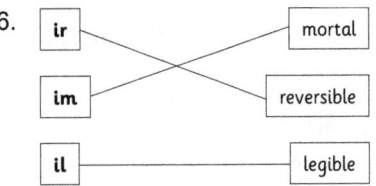

(**1 mark for 1 or 2 correct,
2 marks for 3 correct**)
7. The business was famous for making **peculiar** lamps.
(**1 mark**)
8. preferrence — preference
(**1 mark**)

9. The detective sat me down and asked me to discribe the person who had stolen the bicycle.
   "She was a tall individual with long blonde hair and she looked about fourty years old."
   "Did you see where she went?" the detective asked.
   "She rode the bike through the cemetery."
(**1 mark for 1 correct,
2 marks for both correct**)
10. percieve — perceive
sheild — shield
(**1 mark for 1 correct,
2 marks for both correct**)

Spelling Puzzle – page 40

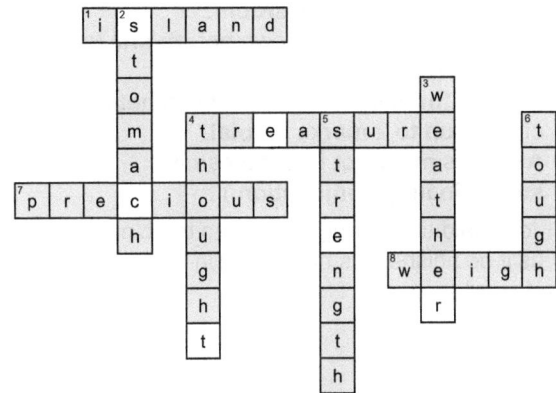

The code word is secret.

Mixed Practice Test 1 – pages 41-43

1. The invitation was addressed to my brother and me.
(**1 mark**)
2. preposition
(**1 mark**)
3. Riley found it hard to sleep because of the icy draught blowing under the door, his incredibly uncomfortable pillow and the furious bird that was squawking at the foot of his bed.
(**1 mark**)

Answers

4.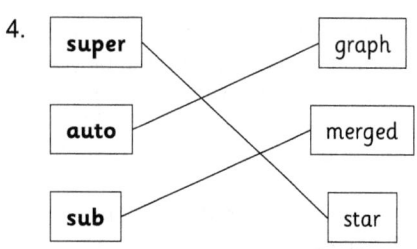

   (**1 mark for 1 or 2 correct,
   2 marks for 3 correct**)

5. I am not allowed to go into my sister's bedroom. After school, we took Charlotte's goldfish to the vet.
   (**1 mark for 1 correct,
   2 marks for both correct**)

6. E.g. My teacher gave me a gold star **because I helped to tidy the classroom.**
   E.g. Maisie mowed the lawn **before she had her dinner.**
   (**1 mark for each sensible subordinate clause, up to 2 marks in total.
   Answers must not use the same subordinating conjunction.**)

7. Josh said that he <u>might</u> come to the cinema with us if he finishes his homework in time.
   (**1 mark**)

8.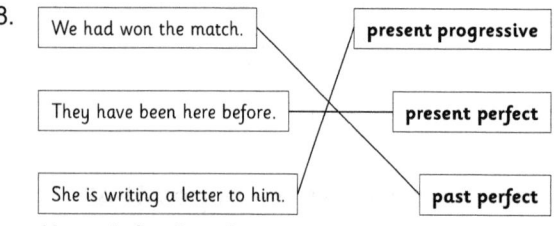

   (**1 mark for 1 or 2 correct,
   2 marks for 3 correct**)

9. Fatima couldn't **believe** her eyes when she saw all the **equipment** in the science laboratory at her new school.
   (**1 mark for 1 correct,
   2 marks for both correct**)

Mixed Practice Test 2 – pages 44-46

1. Mr Bence struggled to contain his intense **anger**.
   (**1 mark**)

2. That hat — the red one — is too small for me.
   (**1 mark**)

3. If the boots don't fit, he can borrow mine.
   (**1 mark**)

4. A donkey trotted past, **whistling** quietly to itself. Darryl poked the pudding **suspiciously**.
   (**1 mark for 1 correct,
   2 marks for both correct**)

5. I am trying to find <u>the</u> seagull that stole <u>my</u> sandwich.
   (**1 mark for 1 correct,
   2 marks for both correct**)

6.
	Noun Phrase	Preposition Phrase
in my bedroom		✓
the big green frog	✓	
behind our recycling box		✓

   (**1 mark for each correct,
   up to 3 marks in total**)

7. During the summer holidays, my family and I love going on <u>adevnsures</u>. Last year, we visited a shark-infested cave at the bottom of the ocean. This year, we are planning an even more extreme experience involving <u>parashutes</u> and dinosaurs.
   (**1 mark for 1 correct,
   2 marks for both correct**)

8. E.g. Megan overslept, so she will **definitely** be late.
   (**1 mark for any sensible adverb that is more certain**)

9. E.g. In the first sentence, the witch often loses her broomstick, but in the second she often flies past my window.
   (**1 mark for any sensible explanation**)

Mixed Practice Test 3 – pages 47-49

1. obay
   (**1 mark**)

Answers

2. Mrs Lang has several unusual pets. The strangest is Kenny, who is a cross between a crocodile and a horse. He looks very unusual indeed.
(1 mark for 1 full stop and 1 capital letter correct, 2 marks for all correct)

3. I like all kinds of music, but percusion is my favourite.
Will your grandad be attendding parents' evening?
**(1 mark for 1 correct,
2 marks for both correct)**

4. These are the gloves <u>that Ruby gave me for Christmas</u>.
Relative pronoun: that
(1 mark for correctly underlining the relative clause, 1 mark for correctly identifying the relative pronoun)

5. Filip got a new bike... — It was bright red...
One day, Filip cycled... — They played two...
On the way home... — A sign said...
**(1 mark for 1 or 2 correct,
2 marks for 3 correct)**

6. I like ham in my sandwiches, but Phoebe prefers jam.
(1 mark)

7. Sarita and Ben **were** playing hockey.
My mum **was** painting the garage.
**(1 mark for 1 correct,
2 marks for both correct)**

8. <u>artifitial</u> — artificial
<u>substance</u> — substance
**(1 mark for 1 correct,
2 marks for both correct)**

Mixed Practice Test 4 – pages 50-52

1. My stepsister (who is an astronaut) lives on Mars.
(1 mark)

2. I made a poster to advert**ise** the school fair.
(1 mark)

3. he
it
**(1 mark for 1 correct,
2 marks for both correct)**

4. Despite the terrible weather, we enjoyed our trip.
(1 mark)

5. <u>admireation</u> — admiration
(1 mark)

6. The elves <u>sometimes</u> get (chilly) in the winter.
**(1 mark for 1 correct,
2 marks for both correct)**

7.
	Co-ordinating Conjunction	Subordinating Conjunction
Kayla went shopping and bought a new mug.	✓	
Before he went swimming, Adam had a snack.		✓
I stroked the cat even though I was scared of it.		✓

**(1 mark for each correct,
up to 3 marks in total)**

8. "I think," yawned Oren, "it's time for bed."
(1 mark)

9. E.g. My mum gives me really good advice.
E.g. I advise you to brush your teeth regularly.
**(1 mark for each sensible sentence,
up to 2 marks in total)**

Mixed Practice Puzzle – page 53

1. brackets, dashes or commas
2. surprise
3. a modal verb
4. knight
5. inverted commas
6. false
7. powerful
8. true

Progress Chart

You've finished all the tests in the book — well done!

Now it's time to put your scores in here
and see how you've done.

	Grammar	Punctuation	Spelling	Mixed Practice
Test 1				
Test 2				
Test 3				
Test 4				
Total				

See if you're on target by checking your total marks for each section in the table below.

Mark	
0-28	You're not quite there yet, but don't worry — keep going back over the questions you find tricky and you'll improve your skills in no time.
29-42	Good job! You're doing really well, but make sure you keep working on your weaker topics.
43-56	Give yourself a huge pat on the back — you're a spelling, punctuation and grammar whizz!